Totally White Room

poems

Gerrit Kouwenaar

Translated by Lloyd Haft

Holland Park Press London

Published by Holland Park Press 2023

Copyright © Gerrit Kouwenaar 2002
Originally published by Querido, Amsterdam

English translation © Lloyd Haft 2023

British Library Cataloguing-in-Publication Data
A catalogue record for this book is available from the British Library

ISBN 978-1-907320-97-2

Cover designed by Reactive Graphics

Printed and bound by
CPI Group (UK) Ltd, Croydon CR0 4YY

www.hollandparkpress.co.uk

CONTENTS

a glass to break

four variations on a triptych

between times

totally white room

a glass to break

A LATTER DAY

It was bound to come: the day it would all
be familiar, grass that was denied came
grumbling again, the hedge spoke up and cut
the view off, the axe needed a grind

that on a latter day one would see the distance again
that the distance was nearer than ever
that one had forgotten the day's year,
that the house had squandered itself, made off, while

one broke into one's innards, the bed
lying unslept and ready, the room emptied
once more forever catching first sight of itself

and that one was cold and ate meat
and that the meat had gone tasteless and the fire
sparked itself and the walls warmed themselves –

WHILE THE DRAGONFLY

While the dragonfly still wet with ink
unfolds his letters on the raised hammer

while the dog unwits itself under the heavenly roof
of the slaughtering block, the moment strikes

while in the ice-cream parlour Bach quits trying
among the timid melting fruit flavours

while the chock-full air between lips and ears
empties into angel grass, counting down the interval

while the light falls asleep in rubble
the silence chokes on a nix between brackets

while the future recedes in white finish, black
speaks again for itself, the evening meat cools

while the now resumes its standstill, sorrow
goes on dripping, the dragonfly not knowing if he lives –

A SPRING

Spring at last, cheered the elder bush in the bloom
of its life after its cankered ancestor
was quietly cremated that winter evening

looking up through his sympathizing outgrowth
he saw the ground of his being touch the sky
in unsure bunches, pale as his marrow

he bloomed what he had outgrown, toadstools
were no concern of his, baby snow was his foretaste
of angelica manna blood-marmalade

at night looking down in the moonlight
he was moved to see
that behind his thin louse-ridden descendant the white
mouldy clubfoot of his father, totally
etherealized, had always been –

A HAPPY CHILDHOOD

Do you ever forget to wind your father's clock?
yes, I do forget to forget my father's time

do you ever put on a straw hat, eye patch, stand-up collar?
no, what I put on is a poem, a gold-leaf summer

do you ever write the last lips to be worded?
yes, I decipher a kiss from mud-spattered roses

do you ever walk through grass that could use mowing?
no, I'm standing still in grass that no one sowed –

WHEN WE WERE STILL YOUNG

When we were still young and the world still old
and we stood on high mountains in a far land
seeing in the valley deep beneath us a long motionless
rusty train, unreally alone
in the eye of a violent void, you cried
while blowing a kiss to the sky
I'm a guidebook, children
teach me to read

and evenings on the square under withering palms
there were wine and olives and a rustling silence
from mournful throats and the darkness pressed
tenderly close to the blade, and you
you bought the unbearable fate of a blind man
and cried the ear drinks

now it's later, an evening years after, the dead
silent train has left, fate's time
has expired, your guidebook is open

under similar older trees I drink
the hoarse voice of your words, I hear your silence –

MUMBLING

Rip paper, sweep rubbish, uncumber love
now that the feed is peacefully simmering,
the beast and the plant

now that myriad birds, blackclouds, stories
write away distance, fold neat as a daily

now that the dried flower denatures in its dust,
the house dog rises above its basket, dries up in its master

this is a flashed message, stained in the kitchen, mumbling
of cut meat, use by date, family silver –

WINTER STANDS STILL

Write winter stands still, read a day without death
spell the snow like a child, melt time
like a clock reflecting itself in ice

it is ice-cold today, so translate what one writes
into a clock that won't run, in the flesh
that is there like snow in the sun

and write how her body was there and bent
supple in flesh and looked back
in the eye of today, and read what this says

the sun on the snow, the child in the sled
the track snowed under, illegible death –

A GLASS TO BREAK

Lying in black in the brightest of rooms
one gathers to the full what the transcript impounds
filling one's contents meekly with void

heaven goes hungry for flesh must be written
one must decompose for language unlives us
articles lungs labials spit

nothing that chimes here is more than a silence
hours repeat themselves never beginning
the moment in search of a glass it could break –

four variations on a triptych

1

The room is open, the windows are closed
a woman studies her given face

she weighs in her mirror whether her lipstick
is fitting in this framed instant

the world is elsewhere, the blind shuts out
all whence and thence with precision

2

While watching thinking up words
all at once there's a different moment

a similar woman in the identical room
spelling the now that elsewhere transpires

is she herself or is she her sister
a rumour that's bare or the back of her muse

3

One recalls how at times on the street
one woman gets lost in another

one looks for words to get the secret
to click in slant rhymes

through an unforeseen hole in the window blind
the muse peers freed into nothing

4

One looks inside in a room
one writes a woman who puts on a stocking

the nylon fingers her skin
is she tugging it on or taking it off

taking it off or tugging it on:
art on the point of being born –

between times

STROLL IN THE PARK

So one walks in on the years, the career, shortness of
breath, step after step lost, avoided

gravel that one kisses with soles, child
where one stumbled, left behind, trapped in a photo

trees un-fleshing names, moonsick dogs, free
minds avid to die, places to throw up, no hope

entrances exits closing nothing, flawed
fruits of freedom, bouquet of the outgrowth,
getaway of the dead –

WORDS ON GLASS

Words on glass, it could hardly be less
one sees right through it as far as the eye longs to say

what speechlessly mirrors betwixt and between
depends on the light, summer or winter

sometimes one sees over lips in amazement
letters appearing as if one breathed them

sometimes they coincide in an instant
thenceforth they're delivered from mirrors

words on glass, but look, it's getting dark
winter spells winter, summer spells summer
time spells time –

POEM MADE OF STONE

I'm lying like a ship by the quay
of a city that's centuries old

I'm anchored to a now
but carry a bygone name

I'm housed between my walls here
like humans inside their skin

space looks out through my windows
I'm structured for humans –

WATER PATH

The way time, lonelier, greets an old friend
wind here caresses lowland and water

behind the dyke peace still gets breath,
ways that weren't there are hurrying slowly

in the house the snap of the golden couple rusts,
the fax rustles, wine shivers in the milk glass

on the grounds the may cherry waves her half-frozen
hands it's spring once again,
soon there'll be lapwings

the herd is already standing outside rougher-coated
a similar sky hangs lower, the sea is a pond

but for whom are preserves fermenting disowned in the
cellar it is written we shall not want
foggy the cities approach in the distance –

POETS MUSICIANS

Poets musicians – at the old fork in the road
they meet again, spelling the names of stars
and stones, whistling on grass blades, cricket psalms

taking in, sizing each other up and addressing,
at times even hugging, awkwardly moved, sharing
as once they did their eyes, their ears, their origins, throats

till once again the milestone points, time overtakes
itself, standstill dismantles itself, the fork stays
itself, the meeting point for good
tinning the moment humming on after, waving –

ONE

That one above all is oneself
in one's bathtub one's war one's mirror

that one above all is one's house
with one's insight one's glasses one's mirror

that one above all one's view
with one's garden one's scythe one's mirror

that one above all one's date
in one's standstill one's failure one's mirror

that one above all one's alter
in one's halfhood one's whole skin one's mirror

that one above all is of flesh
on one's sofa one's notepad one's plate –

BETWEEN TIMES

The unmouthed ear of this poem
hears deafer by the word, silence
protruding under ground

nowhere an answer, unsayable questions, continues to
torment the hasty moment, be the light
near-sighted already, the flesh yet undying –

totally white room

WORDS LIKE THESE

What did you smell like, then, it was
a word that wasn't, summersnow, semblance
of lightweave, lipsilence, honeygrass

today, autumn, in our sloppily cared-for paradise
I heard, impartial, through the overgrowth
the jingling of your pathetically muffled silver

seeing, I cried for the deafest, white moths, life
so light no name could hold it, and you
set this dispossessed moment to being, me to trembling

words like these stand still for good, I
dwell in them, even now as the wind rises,
branches of old shadows break and you're cold –

TOTALLY WHITE ROOM

Let's make the room white one more time
one more time the totally white room, you, me

this won't save time, but one more time
make the room white, now, never again later

we'll almost echo perfection
our lines more white than legible

so one more time that room, once and for all total
the way we lay there, lie, shall lie there
more white than, together –

MIND, WORD

Mind, word, inediblest of fleshes, airish
as the seepage in speech, take on
memory's black, the hole in the ground

answer the sigh of the stilled dog
make your sense of the senseless verse of the cricket
the deaf disearthed unheavened ground –

NOT WRITTEN

That you walk through the house
murmur in my darkness, instilling your silence,
laying it out, eating it up in me, no
that can't be true, can't be said
can't be heard, be written

your full-bodied absence surrounds, so extra-
mortal the way the clothes hang anew
that your cold feet hold these steps of mine
on the worn stilled treads
of the defenceless down stairway

eater come eat at last, meat
was always your favourite, the glass
fills time, the bread
remains the hunger, the only –

IN THE ORCHARD

Poet, I'm here again for a moment, jolted
awake in you, I'm walking with you
through the stilled future of our past

it's all overgrown, this life is
beyond help, it's all there
everywhere in twilight, light without sky, is this
a photo, where is the ground, where is
the stone where the dog breathed last

you're sitting at the window, I have a clear vision
of what I'm not seeing, a body bound up
in its standstill, its words

we once saw a stone in a glass case
as the silent resounding semblance,
the lasting sense of a bread

poet, nothing rhymes with dead, I'm stroking
the denatured velvet of my nightdress, I'm going
to sleep in you again –

WHEN WE

When we made up again
remember how it clicked, when our halves
chimed again true, words by candlelight

and how we lay translated, spelled in old flesh
breath lifting us away, straw fire ignited us

happiness hung like smoke about us, outside
the minor cold of autumn, we were satisfied

so laid-out in what we possessed, the moment
embraced us, then time set in

one still hears a ticking behind the whitewash, hollow
slowly falling mouldy black drops –

POÈME, LANCÔME

The leaving behind, the forgotten, the things
that yield speechless, the insightful
the fugitive, the remnant

while the poem dries, re-reads itself
one sees through oneself by the glass of one's mind
a smell of perfection cut off in its void

now one must unsense with eyes by the mouthful
count oneself, halve, grow volatile in postscript
pale away in daylight, waste away in body linen

so one can leave oneself behind, thinner and less
outward the point in time, so one can lay oneself aside
in eaten-into food, as grammar gives in –

SO PEACEFUL THE EVENING

While the last poem eats up the moment
the maker stands up drained from the table
he cleans his carving knife and looks out the window

on the flagstones the leaves breathing their last
relieved of their summer, the wind angel crouching
in the eternal weeds waiting for time

so peaceful the evening of wars and farewells
world, truth and love comprising invulnerably
their iron letters

and now for something edible, blooded white bread
then finally to sleep, black is in fashion –

.

ACKNOWLEDGEMENTS

totally white room, *so it's a peaceful evening*, *a happy childhood*, *when we*, and *poème, lancôme* have previously appeared in the Gerrit Kouwenaar brochure in the series *Contemporary Dutch Poets*, issued by the Foundation for the Production and Translation of Dutch Literature (Amsterdam, n.d.).

The same poems were published for Poetry International in 2003.

winter stands still was published in:
In a Different Light: Fourteen Contemporary Dutch-Language Poets, ed. Rob Schouten and Robert Minhinnick, Seren, 2002
The Low Countries: Arts and Society in Flanders and The Netherlands, Ons Erfdeel, 2000
Revolver 106 (27:1), 2000

Several poems were published for Poetry International, June 1999.

THE AUTHOR

Gerrit Kouwenaar, 1923-2014, is one of the foremost Dutch poets. He also was an author, translator and journalist.

During the Second Word War he was active in the resistance, was arrested and subsequently went into hiding. He made his debut with *Vroege voorjaarsdag* (*Early Spring Day*), a clandestine self-published poetry collection.

His official debut collection *Achter een woord* (*Behind One Word*) was published in 1953, and he became one of the leading lights in the 1950s movement *De Vijftigers*, a group of experimental poets influenced by the COBRA avant-garde movement. His reputation grew and by the 1980s, he not only had acquired a large loyal set of readers, but also influenced many Dutch poets.

He won all the major Dutch language poetry and literature prizes including, in 1970, the PC Hooft Prize for his entire oeuvre, and in 1989 the Dutch Literature Prize, again for his entire oeuvre. He also translated plays by Brecht, Goethe and Sartre. In 2009, the Society of Dutch Literature named Kouwenaar the recipient of its annual honour.

His poetry collection *Totaal witte kamer* (*Totally White Room*) was published by Querido in 2002. It won the Karel van de Woestijne prize in 2004 and the KANTL prize in 2005.

THE TRANSLATOR

Lloyd Haft (1946) is an American-born Dutch poet, translator and sinologist. In 1968 he graduated from Harvard College and moved to Leiden to complete his MA in 1973 and his PhD in 1981. From 1973 to 2004 he taught Chinese language and literature, mostly poetry, at Leiden University.

He has widely translated poetry into English from the Dutch and the Chinese, including works by Gerrit Kouwenaar, Anna Enquist, HH ter Balkt, Lo Fu, Yang Lingye, Bian Zhilin and Zhou Mengdie.

Since the 1980s he has also been active as a poet writing in Dutch and English. He was awarded the Jan Campert Prize for his 1993 bilingual volume *Atlantis* (Querido, 1993) and the Ida Gerhardt Prize for his 2003 Dutch free-verse readings of the Psalms (republished by Vesuvius in 2011).

His latest book of poetry in Dutch is *Intocht* (*Introit*), issued by the American Book Center in June 2018. His recent translations include *Herman Gorter: Selected Poems* (Arimei, 2021) and *Zhou Mengdie: 41 Poems* (Azoth, 2022).

The publisher and assistant have worked closely with Lloyd Haft on his remarkable translation of Gerrit Kouwenaar's masterpiece *Totally White Room*.

Holland Park Press, founded in 2009, is a privately-owned independent company publishing literary fiction: novels, novellas, short stories; and poetry. The company is run by brother and sister team Arnold and Bernadette Jansen op de Haar, who publish an author not just a book. Holland Park Press specialises in finding new literary talent by accepting unsolicited manuscripts from authors all year round and by running competitions. It has been successful in giving older authors a chance to make their debut and in raising the profile of Dutch authors in translation.

To

Learn more about Gerrit Kouwenaar & Lloyd Haft
Discover other interesting books
Read our blogs and news items
Find out how to submit your manuscript
Take part in one of our competitions

Visit www.hollandparkpress.co.uk

Bookshop: http://www.hollandparkpress.co.uk/books.php

Holland Park Press in the social media:

https://www.twitter.com/HollandParkPres
https://www.facebook.com/HollandParkPress
https://www.linkedin.com/company/holland-park-press
https://www.youtube.com/user/HollandParkPress
https://www.instagram.com/hollandparkpress/